T0384376

HOW TO BE A DETECTIVE

AND OTHER CRIME-FIGHTING JOBS

WRITTEN BY
DETECTIVE ALEXANDRA BEEVER

ILLUSTRATED BY
SOL LINERO

POLICE LINE DO NOT CROSS /// POLICE LINE DO NOT CROSS /// POLICE

nosy crow

To Imogen—for a curious person, life is an adventure
waiting to be discovered—and to Lillie, whose curiosity
kindled dreams she lived and loved by.
— A.B.

To my curious little kids, Ulises and Eloisa. Love, Mom
— S.L.

First published in 2023 by Nosy Crow Ltd
Wheat Wharf, 27a Shad Thames,
London, SE1 2XZ, UK

This edition published 2024 by Nosy Crow Inc.
145 Lincoln Road, Lincoln, MA 01773, USA

www.nosycrow.us

ISBN 979-8-88777-080-2

Nosy Crow and associated logos are trademarks
and/or registered trademarks of Nosy Crow Ltd.

Used under license.

Text © 2023 by Alexandra Beever
Illustrations © 2023 by Sol Linero

Library of Congress Catalog Card Number pending.

Printed in China following rigorous ethical sourcing standards.

Papers used by Nosy Crow are made from wood grown in sustainable forests.

10 9 8 7 6 5 4 3 2 1

CONTENTS

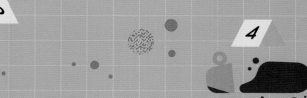

WHAT IS A DETECTIVE?

You might have read about detectives in books or seen them in movies and on TV, hunting for clues and solving mysteries. But what are detectives?

A detective is a police officer with special training whose job it is to investigate crimes. Using their skills and knowledge, detectives uncover the truth about crimes in order to find the people responsible for them.

Police detectives have to investigate and solve all kinds of crimes, from **forging documents** and **theft** to people **being hurt by someone** or **disappearing**.

POLICE

POLICE

POLICE LINE DO NOT

POLICE L

2

DO NOT CROSS   POLICE LINE DO NOT CROSS   POLICE LINE DO NOT CROSS   PO

1

Detectives spend a lot of time speaking with the people who were affected by a crime (**victims**) and anyone who saw a crime happen (**witnesses**). They also interview people who they think might have committed a crime (**suspects**).

DID YOU KNOW?
The word "detective" comes from the Latin word *detectus,* which means to uncover the truth.

A detective's office is inside a **police station.** There is a lot of private information stored there, so it's important that it is kept secure and members of the public are not allowed to enter.

Police detectives need some special equipment to help them with their job:

Identification to prove that they are a detective.

A **police radio** to call for help or ask for extra officers.

Disposable gloves to wear at crime scenes to keep evidence from being damaged.

A **notebook and pen** to take notes.

A **cell phone** to take pictures of evidence and contact people.

WHY DO
WE NEED DETECTIVES?

Police officers are always working to protect people in order to make our communities safer places to live in. But some crimes are more serious and complicated than others, so we need detectives to solve them.

It is the detective's job to collect as much information as possible to solve the crime. This is called a **criminal investigation** and the material collected is called **evidence**. Evidence can be anything from a fingerprint to a blood stain. It must all be collected and recorded correctly by the detective, since it could hold the key to cracking the case.

Detectives are experts at **finding clues** and **figuring out what story they tell.** People leave lots of evidence behind, even if they are trying hard not to be caught committing a crime. Some of it might not seem important to ordinary people, but detectives are trained to collect many small clues and piece them all together, sort of like solving a giant jigsaw puzzle.

Often, crimes are not as simple as they seem. Sometimes criminals work in groups, known as **Organized Crime Groups (OCGs),** and we need the skills of detectives to identify them. Some undercover officers even wear disguises and pretend to be members of a criminal group. They can watch and listen for evidence to help the police catch these criminals.

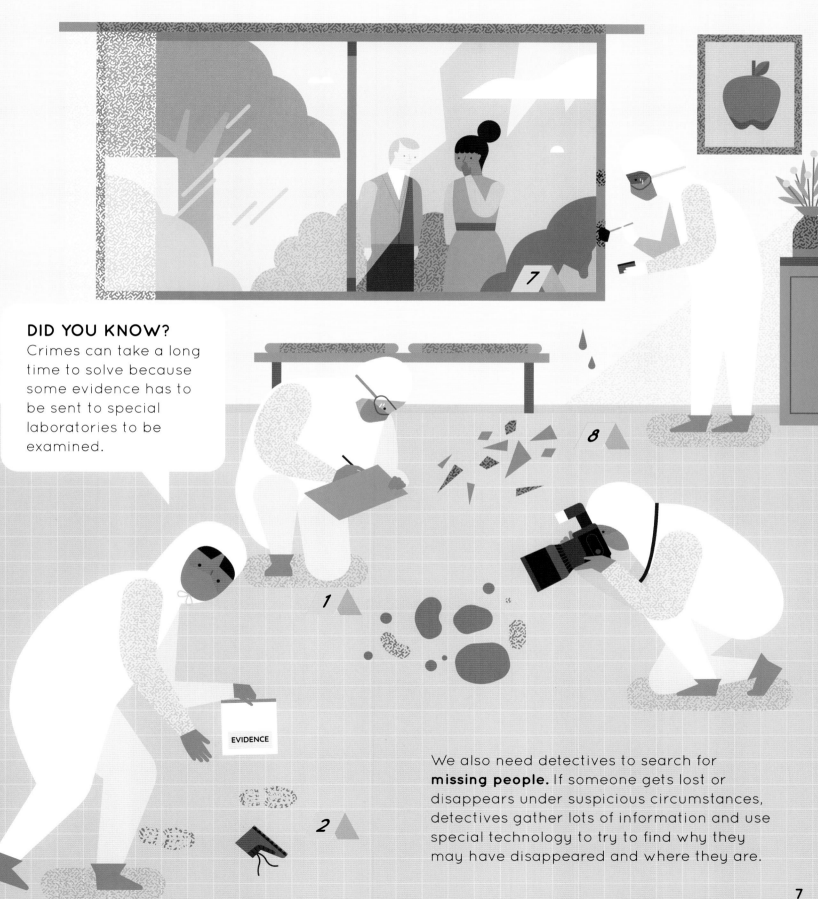

DID YOU KNOW?
Crimes can take a long time to solve because some evidence has to be sent to special laboratories to be examined.

We also need detectives to search for **missing people.** If someone gets lost or disappears under suspicious circumstances, detectives gather lots of information and use special technology to try to find why they may have disappeared and where they are.

THE HISTORY OF
DETECTIVES

People have been fighting crime and trying to solve mysteries for thousands of years, but when did detectives first appear?

The first private detective agency was founded in Paris by Eugène François Vidocq, a French detective who used to be a criminal.

Kate Warne, a member of the Pinkerton Detective Agency, became the first female detective in the world.

Sir Howard Vincent published his *Police Code*, which said that no one should touch a dead body or crime scene before the police arrive.

| 1833 | 1841 | 1856 | 1879 | 1881 | 1892 |

The first detective story, *The Murders in the Rue Morgue* by Edgar Allan Poe, was published.

Alphonse Bertillon, a French criminologist, invented the Bertillon System. By recording body measurements and facial features of criminals, he was able to identify hundreds of repeat criminals.

The Adventures of Sherlock Holmes by Arthur Conan Doyle was published. Sherlock Holmes is the world's most famous fictional detective.

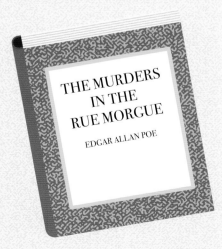

THE MURDERS IN THE RUE MORGUE

EDGAR ALLAN POE

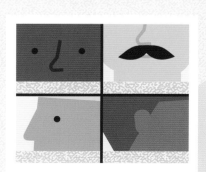

DID YOU KNOW?
DNA can be found at crime scenes in blood, skin cells, hair, and saliva. It is unique to each person and often criminals don't realize they have left it behind.

Fingerprints were used as evidence for the first time. The case took place in West Bengal, India.

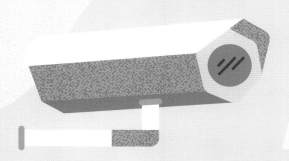

A German engineer called Walter Bruch designed the first video surveillance camera.

For the first time, someone was convicted (found guilty) of murder using DNA evidence.

1898	1935	1942	1976	1988	2000

The first training course for detectives opened in the US. Some of the first countries to send officers to it were China, Canada, and Great Britain.

Automatic License Plate Recognition (ALPR) was invented though it was not widely used in the US until the 2000s. It allows detectives to track criminals using the license plates on their cars.

Drones began to be used by the police. Drones are small, uncrewed aircraft guided by remote control, used for surveillance and to help search for people or objects.

1MO G3N

HOW DO YOU
BECOME A DETECTIVE?

**Good detectives are nosy and inquisitive. They want to find out about everything!
And they put a lot of time and effort into discovering as much information as possible.**

It is really important that detectives can **communicate well,** so working hard in school
at **reading and writing** is helpful for anyone who wants to become a detective.
But detectives need lots of other skills too . . .

Detectives must be **fair.**
They have to treat the
people they meet with
respect and try to see
things from everyone's
point of view, including
the suspects'.

Detectives also have to be **patient.**
It can take a long time to collect
all the evidence together and
figure out who the perpetrator is.
A detective must be careful not to
rush an investigation so that vital
evidence isn't missed.

Some detectives need
to look at graphs, take
measurements, or solve
equations during their
investigations, so having
good **math skills** can
help them.

**Understanding different religions
and traditions,** as well as being
able to **speak different languages,**
are really useful skills to have as
a detective. We need detectives
from many different cultures
and backgrounds so that crimes
can be investigated fairly and
respectfully.

Detectives are great at **observing,** or noticing, and **remembering things.** They ask lots of questions, such as:

How tall was the person?

When was the last time the person was seen?

How did that footprint get there?

What was that person wearing?

Where did the person go when they left the house?

Where did the fingerprints on that window come from?

Who left that door open?

To practice these skills, you can look for clues and evidence while you are out. After all, anything could be evidence of a crime . . .

Follow footprints in the mud. They can be human tracks or animal tracks. What do you think that person or animal was doing there?

Practice writing down what you noticed earlier in the day. What did you see, hear, smell, touch, and taste?

Memorize license plates. Who was driving the car? How many people were in it? Where were they going?

So, you are nosy, patient, and good at observing and remembering things? You have all the right skills to become a detective! But there's a lot of **training** to do first . . .

WHAT
TRAINING DOES A DETECTIVE NEED?

In most places, to become a police detective, you need at least some college education. You don't have to focus on any particular subject, but aspiring detectives often get a degree in **criminal justice**. **Criminology** (the study of crime), **psychology** (the study of the mind), and **legal studies** (the study of law and the court system) are other useful topics to learn about.

The path to becoming a **police detective** and the qualifications you will need vary widely from state to state and department to department, but the first step after college is always to complete training at a **police academy** and to apply to become a **uniformed police officer**. Then you need to gain lots of on-the-job experience, working with detectives to learn how to deal with the public, process crime scenes, and conduct investigations.

Finally, it's helpful to get an **official certification** by taking a test that shows you are ready to be a detective. Even with an official certification, it takes most officers several years of hard work and gaining experience before they are promoted to detective.

POLICE

POLICE

Officers hoping to become detectives work alongside experienced detectives, learning the **key skills** they need to solve a case.

Sometimes evidence or clues can be difficult to understand. Aspiring detectives need to develop good **problem-solving skills** to decode these clues and find a possible answer to the puzzle.

Computer and technology skills help a detective to record information and understand the devices, programs, and apps that criminals might use.

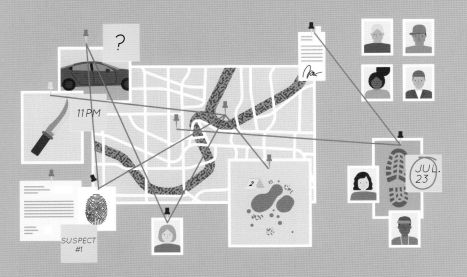

Over time, officers who hope to become detectives learn to pick up on **behavior and body language.** By studying the way someone speaks or uses their eyes, hands, or legs, detectives can figure out if the suspect is lying or hiding a key piece of information.

Using all these skills, officers have to show that they can **investigate** all sorts of crimes before they they can be promoted to detective.

WHAT HAPPENS WHEN A CRIME IS REPORTED TO THE POLICE?

When someone calls 911 to report a crime, they will speak to a dispatcher. The dispatcher's job is to ask lots of questions and decide how many police officers need to be sent out and if any other help is needed.

Police in uniform are often the first to arrive at the crime scene. They will assess the situation and maintain contact with the 911 operator. If someone has been injured, they will give them **first aid** until an **ambulance** arrives.

DID YOU KNOW?
Detectives sometimes have to work late into the night and on weekends when they are working on a case.

Police officers make sure that **everyone is safe** and that **none of the evidence is disturbed.** It's important that it not be removed, lost, or contaminated (damaged). They also need to find out the **names of the victim and witnesses** and identify the **suspect.** These actions are the **building blocks** of the investigation.

POLICE LINE DO NOT CROSS ///// POLICE LINE DO NOT CROSS ///// P

Police officers put up **crime tape** to make sure that no one enters or contaminates the crime scene. Then they **speak to witnesses,** write down **descriptions of suspects** and **vehicle license plates,** and look for **cameras** that may have recorded what has happened.

At this stage, a **detective** will be put in charge of the investigation. They visit the scene to make sure that all the evidence has been collected and start to think about who the **suspect** might be. Using their previous experience with similar crimes, they look for a **motive,** or reason why the crime has happened.

The most important time in an investigation is right after a crime has been committed, when there is still a lot of evidence at the scene. Detectives have to make the most of this time, **before evidence is lost** and **people's memories become hazy.**

Detectives spend a lot of time talking to witnesses and taking **witness statements,** recording what they have seen and heard. But there is still a lot of other evidence to find . . .

HOW DOES A DETECTIVE LOOK FOR CLUES?

A good detective has an open mind and looks for clues everywhere. They know that an object, smell, or even something someone says could help to identify the person responsible for a crime.

A specially trained officer called a **Crime Scene Investigator (CSI)** will go to the scene with the detective. They are experts at looking for **evidence that is hard to find,** such as fingerprints, blood, strands of hair, and even bullets. They can also figure out what sort of **tools** have been used to break into a building by looking at the marks left behind.

POLICE

EVIDENCE

Clues can also be found on **cell phones.** Detectives can find out who has contacted the victim or suspect and even where the phone was when it was used. Cell phones also contain lots of other evidence like photographs, emails, and what a person has been looking up on the internet.

POLICE LINE DO NOT CROSS

POLICE LINE DO NOT CROSS

There are usually plenty of **surveillance cameras** in public places, recording 24 hours a day. Detectives look through hours of footage to figure out where the suspect was before the crime and where they went afterward. Sometimes cameras even capture the crime itself.

Many of our roads and parking lots also have **ALPR cameras.** These cameras can read license plates to identify cars that have been near to or at the crime scene.

DID YOU KNOW?
Detectives can use **trained detection dogs** to sniff out any evidence that was left behind at the scene, like clothing or weapons.

Detectives can get a good idea of what the suspect looks like using **computer technology.** Some police departments use **special software** to create an electronic picture of the suspect's face from information given by witnesses.

If a detective thinks they have found the person who has committed the crime, they might set up a **police lineup** to be certain. This is when the victim or witness is shown photos of the suspect with photos of several other people who look like the accused person. The victim or witness must then identify the suspect.

Once a detective has found enough evidence to be reasonably sure the suspect is guilty, they will arrest them . . .

WHAT HAPPENS WHEN YOU
FIND A SUSPECT?

When a detective has found their suspect, they can make an arrest. Being arrested means that the suspect has to go with the detective to the police station to be interviewed.

A detective can make an arrest if they witness a person committing a crime. They can also arrest someone if they have **probable cause,** or suspicion based on facts, that the person has committed a crime, or if the officer has an **arrest warrant,** which is permission from a judge to arrest a suspect.

At the police station, the suspect is **booked.** Their **fingerprints** and in some cases a **sample of their saliva** are taken to see if they match any of the samples taken from the **crime scene.** A **mug shot,** or a photo, is also taken of their face and profile.

The suspect is allowed to **speak with a lawyer** who advises them on how to answer the officers' questions and makes sure their rights are being protected.

While this is happening, the detective prepares to **interview the suspect.**
In the interview, they will ask the suspect lots of questions to find out what
happened, such as:

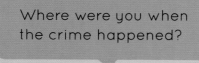

Where were you when
the crime happened?

Who were
you with?

What were you wearing?

Why did
you do it?

How did
you do it?

DID YOU KNOW?
If a suspect does
not want to answer
a detective's question,
they have the **right to
remain silent.**

The interview is
recorded so that it
can be watched by
anyone else involved
in the investigation.

After the booking process, the suspect is charged with the crime or crimes.
They are then usually given the opportunity to **post bail,** or pay a set amount
of money so they can be released until their trial date, when they go to court . . .

WHAT HAPPENS WHEN A
PERSON GOES TO COURT?

When a suspect is charged with a crime, it means that there is enough evidence to suggest that they may be guilty, but a jury has to make the final decision.

Court is where all the evidence in an investigation is presented to a judge and jury, and the jury must determine if the **defendant** (suspect) is guilty or innocent. Each side has the chance to tell their version of what happened.

Disagreements that are between two people or groups of people, or between people and a company, go to **civil court**. Bigger crimes, such as **robberies** and **murders**, where police detectives are involved, are considered crimes against not just the victim but against society as a whole. These cases are tried in **criminal court**.

Before the trial, the police detective **helps the prosecutor understand the evidence** so the prosecutor can build their case. In court, the detective **testifies,** or presents the evidence to the court. Lawyers from both sides **ask the detective questions** to help the jury **understand what the evidence is** and **how it was gathered.**

Lawyers for the prosecution, or **prosecutors,** make the case against the defendant. They explain what happened to the victim and present evidence that supports their claim that the defendant is guilty.

Defense lawyers present the defendant's point of view. Their goal is to show that the defendant is innocent.

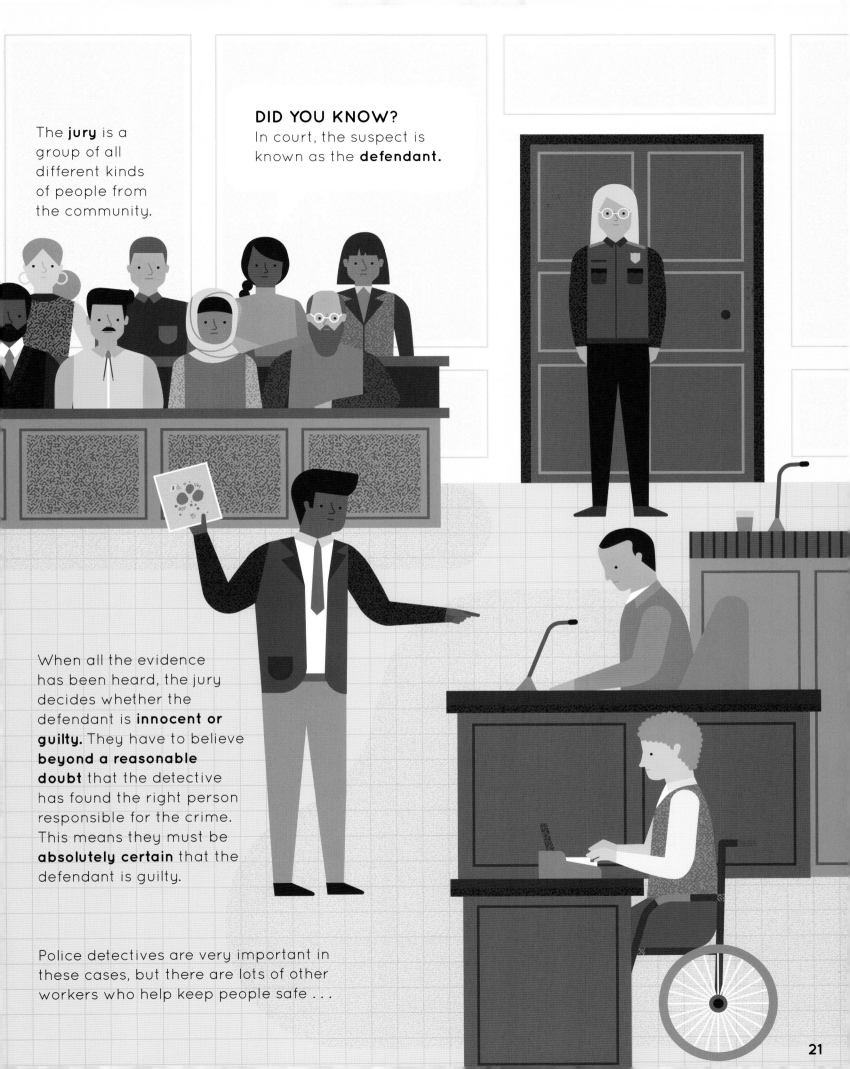

The **jury** is a group of all different kinds of people from the community.

DID YOU KNOW?
In court, the suspect is known as the **defendant.**

When all the evidence has been heard, the jury decides whether the defendant is **innocent or guilty.** They have to believe **beyond a reasonable doubt** that the detective has found the right person responsible for the crime. This means they must be **absolutely certain** that the defendant is guilty.

Police detectives are very important in these cases, but there are lots of other workers who help keep people safe . . .

21

WHAT OTHER CRIME-FIGHTING JOBS ARE THERE?

Private detectives can be hired by a private person or company. They don't work for the police or the government, but they may investigate personal, legal, or financial information about someone or help find missing people. They do this by searching through bank details, public records, and computer databases and conducting interviews.

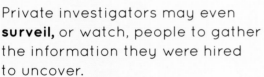

JAN 22 ✓

243 34   CALL 5PM

Private investigators may even **surveil,** or watch, people to gather the information they were hired to uncover.

Sometimes this involves following people, and blending into crowds or hiding so that they are not seen by the people they are watching.

22

The Secret Service protects the president and vice president and leaders visiting from other countries. They also investigate financial crimes committed against the US. Celebrities and other public figures often hire **bodyguards**, or **personal protection officers**, to keep them safe.

A **SWAT** (Special Weapons and Tactics) team is a specialized police unit that uses **military methods** to respond to serious incidents, where people are armed with knives, guns, or other weapons.

The Federal Bureau of Investigation, or **FBI,** prevents and solves crimes, such as **cybercrime** and **organized crime,** that threaten the safety of the whole country. They gather and analyze intelligence (information), and perform law enforcement duties.

DO YOU LIKE
VEHICLES?
THEN ONE OF THESE JOBS MIGHT BE FOR YOU.

Sometimes police officers or specialist teams have to use vehicles, such as cars, motorcycles, boats, or helicopters. Driving these vehicles safely and properly requires lots of training.

Most police officers are trained to drive very powerful cars or motorcycles at high speeds to help catch criminals. They have to be highly skilled drivers to avoid causing any injury to members of the public. Sometimes they drive unmarked police cars, which look like normal cars until their sirens and flashing lights are turned on. This helps to catch criminals unaware!

Many organizations provide **Search and Rescue (SAR),** finding and helping people who are missing and in danger. They often use boats and take diving equipment with them to explore underwater.

Some SAR specialists also have skills such as mountaineering or potholing (traveling through underground caves). All SAR workers need to be able to give first aid to injured people.

Law enforcement pilots and some SAR team members fly **helicopters,** which can travel quickly to places that are difficult to access, like mountains or woods. They can also hover over large events or crime scenes, or find missing people and criminals in the dark using a searchlight or thermal imaging cameras, which detect body heat.

SAR teams also work with the **U.S. Coast Guard,** the branch of the military that patrols the oceans, using their knowledge and equipment to save lives and fight crime.

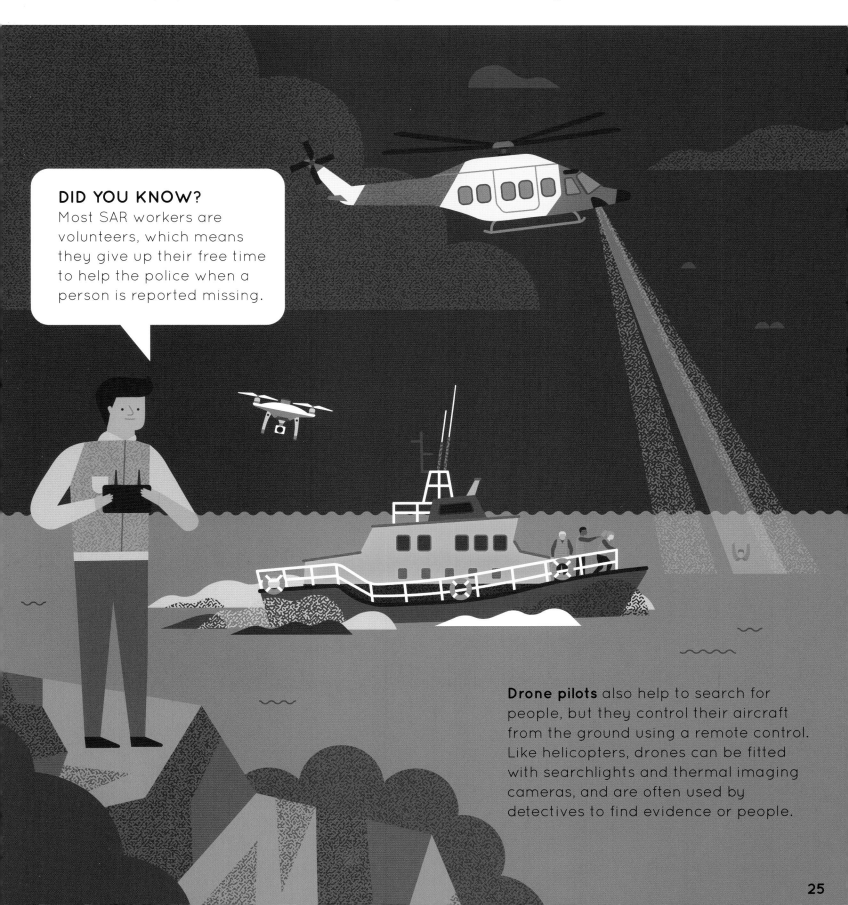

DID YOU KNOW?
Most SAR workers are volunteers, which means they give up their free time to help the police when a person is reported missing.

Drone pilots also help to search for people, but they control their aircraft from the ground using a remote control. Like helicopters, drones can be fitted with searchlights and thermal imaging cameras, and are often used by detectives to find evidence or people.

WHAT ABOUT A JOB IN CRIMINAL SCIENCE?

Detectives often need help from scientists in order to solve a crime.

Forensic pathologists, or medical examiners, are specially trained doctors who examine the bodies of people who have died suddenly, unexpectedly, or violently to determine how, and sometimes when, they may have died.

DID YOU KNOW?
A forensic pathologist must undergo several years of additional training after earning a medical degree.

Forensic entomologists study insects found in and near dead bodies. They understand the life cycles of different insects and the role they play in decomposition, or how dead bodies break down. Using this information, they can help to figure out the time a person died.

EVIDENCE

1

Forensic scientists visit crime scenes with detectives and gather as much evidence as possible. They carefully package up the evidence and take it to a laboratory for testing.

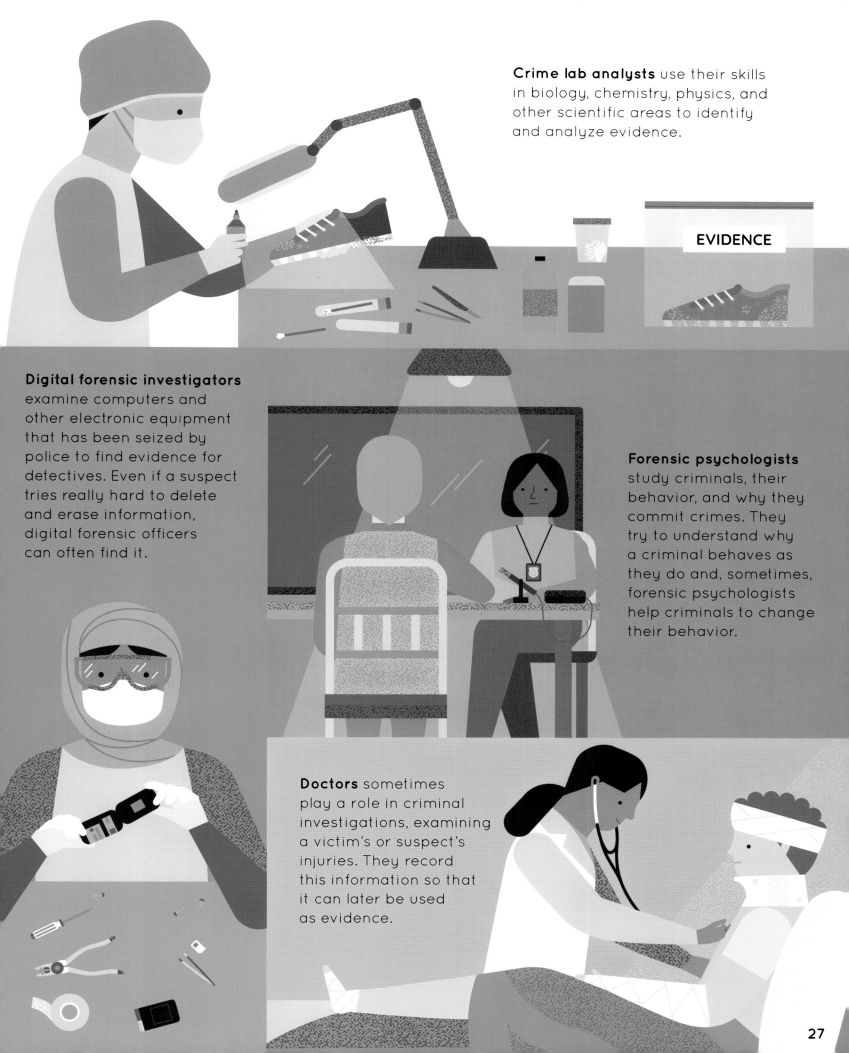

Crime lab analysts use their skills in biology, chemistry, physics, and other scientific areas to identify and analyze evidence.

EVIDENCE

Digital forensic investigators examine computers and other electronic equipment that has been seized by police to find evidence for detectives. Even if a suspect tries really hard to delete and erase information, digital forensic officers can often find it.

Forensic psychologists study criminals, their behavior, and why they commit crimes. They try to understand why a criminal behaves as they do and, sometimes, forensic psychologists help criminals to change their behavior.

Doctors sometimes play a role in criminal investigations, examining a victim's or suspect's injuries. They record this information so that it can later be used as evidence.

ARE YOU GOOD AT
GATHERING INFORMATION AND KEEPING SECRETS?
THEN TRY ONE OF THESE JOBS.

Some people work for **intelligence agencies,** such as the **Central Intelligence Agency,** or **CIA.** The CIA works hard to protect the country and everyone who lives in it from **terrorism** and **espionage.**

They do this by collecting and analyzing **intelligence,** or information, about foreign countries and their citizens to help keep the United States safe.

The **CIA** and the **FBI** are both intelligence-gathering organizations run by the government. The CIA works mostly outside the US and focuses on threats from foreign countries, while the FBI works mostly inside the US and also enforces federal (national) laws in addition to gathering intelligence.

Undercover law-enforcement agents are police officers who join crime organizations and build up relationships with their members to gather information about their criminal activity. They have to be very careful to hide their true identity.

Internal Affairs is a division of a law enforcement agency that makes sure that detectives and police officers are performing their duties properly and fairly.

WHAT ABOUT THE
MORE UNUSUAL CRIME-FIGHTING JOBS?

Do you like dogs? Then you could work as a **canine trainer** for law enforcement, teaching dogs how to follow commands and use their sense of smell to find missing people or evidence of illegal activity.

Self-defense instructors teach people how to protect themselves if they are attacked or assaulted.

Financial investigators work to uncover fraud (criminal dishonesty), embezzlement (a kind of theft), and other financial crimes.

Fingerprint analysts are highly skilled at collecting, examining, and analyzing fingerprints as well as palm prints and footprints.

Handwriting experts examine and analyze handwriting samples and signatures to determine if two or more documents were written or signed by the same person.

If you are interested in horse-riding, you could become a **mounted police officer.** They keep large crowds of people safe at events like parades and protests.

Some ski resorts hire **police on skis** to assist ski patrol and help keep their slopes safe.

If you love drawing, then you could become a **forensic artist.** They work with detectives to create sketches of suspects and victims to help in their identification. They also create drawings and models of crime scenes.

DID YOU KNOW?
Some forensic artists can create a digital image to show how a missing person might look years after they went missing.

GET INVOLVED!

If you would like to learn more about becoming a detective or fighting crime, there are many things you can do . . .

You can practice your detective skills by looking for footprints or fingerprints, memorizing license plates, and analyzing and comparing handwriting samples. You can also see if your school has any language or coding classes that you could take.

You can even start your own detective agency with friends and offer to help classmates or family members by searching for their missing belongings or solving other mysteries. Keep a notebook so that you can write down all the clues your agency finds and any statements from witnesses you interview.

All you really need is a passion for helping people and fighting crime!

ORGANIZATIONS TO EXPLORE:

Spy Museum Activities https://www.spymuseum.org/education-programs/kids-families/activities/
Make Your Own Detective Kit https://www.wikihow.com/Make-a-Detective-Kit
CIA Spy Kids https://www.cia.gov/spy-kids/
CSI Detective Activities https://csi.webadventures.games/en/For-Educators/Online-Activities.html